Attention Deficit Disorder

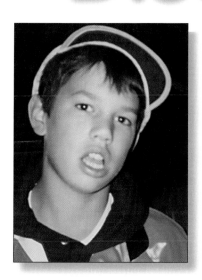

SUSAN DUDLEY GOLD

Expert Reviews by Priscilla L. Vail, and Robert L. Johnson, M.D.

Enslow Publishers, Inc.

40 Industrial Road   PO Box 38
Box 398   Aldershot
Berkeley Heights, NJ 07922 Hants GU12 6BP
USA   UK

http://www.enslow.com

Dedicated to Christopher Prosser, who will succeed no matter what, and to his mother, Sharon Prosser, who, with patience, kindness, and love, teaches and guides our children, with and without ADD

Acknowledgments
With thanks to:
Priscilla Vail, M.A.T., learning specialist and author of several books on learning, for her advice and review of this book.
Christopher Prosser and the Prosser family for sharing their story.
Lindy Holt for suggestions, insight, and additions to the book and for her leadership in the Maine ADD support group.
Dr. Edward Hallowell for his words of encouragement.
Neil Broere and John Gold for providing photographs for this book.

Library of Congress Cataloging-in-Publication Data
Gold, Susan Dudley.
    Attention deficit disorder / Susan Dudley Gold; expert review by Priscilla L. Vail.
        p. cm. —— (Health watch)
    Includes bibliographical references and index.
    Summary: Discusses the causes, symptoms, diagnosis, and treatment of attention deficit disorder, as well as ways in which people live with it.
    ISBN 0-7660-1657-9 (hardcover)
    1. Attention deficit-hyperactivity disorder—Juvenile literature.
[1. Attention-deficit hyperactivity disorder.] I. Vail, Priscilla L. II. Title. III. Health watch (Berkeley Heights, N.J.)
    RJ506.H9 G636 2000b
    618.92'8589—dc21
                              00-008383
Printed in the United States of America

10 9 8 7 6 5 4 3 2 1

To Our Readers:
All internet addresses in this book were active and appropriate when we went to press. Any comments or suggestions can be sent by e-mail to Comments@enslow.com or to the address on the back cover.

Illustration and Photo Credits:
© John C. Gold: pp. 1, 4, 11, 12, 15, 32; © PhotoDisc, Inc.: pp. 7, 21, 24, 27, 28, 31, 36; © Digital Stock, Corbis Corp.: p. 19; © Jill K. Gregory, p. 18; © Neil Broere, courtesy Christopher Prosser, p. 39.

Cover Illustrations:
Large photo, © John Gold; illustration, © Jill K. Gregory; inset, © Digital Stock, Corbis Corp.

Contents

Christopher Prosser, who has attention deficit disorder, enjoys canoeing and the challenges of outdoor living.

Chapter 1

Chris's Story

Four-year-old Christopher Prosser decided to have a little fun one evening. While his father was at work and his mother fed his infant brother, Chris unlocked the door, unchained the dog, and ran down to the beach near the family's home. His mother, Sharon Prosser, soon discovered Chris was gone. In a panic she called a neighbor to watch the baby and then ran along the path leading to the beach.

What she saw at the end of the path frightened her even more. There in the sand lay Chris's shoes and socks. She peered into the waves but saw no one. Frantically she ran along the beach, looking for some trace of her little boy. Several hundred yards away she saw two forms against the darkening sky. As she drew closer, she could see the black figures were Chris and his dog. Chris was sitting on a log, chatting to himself and drawing circles in the sand. "Hi, Mom," he shouted happily to his mother. "We've been waiting for you."

This was one of many episodes that delighted Chris and

scared his parents almost to death. Chris has **attention deficit disorder (ADD)**, a brain disorder that makes it hard for people to pay attention. People with the disorder often engage in risky behavior, act without thinking, and are full of energy.

Chris is one of about 4 million American children who have ADD. It is the most common childhood brain disorder, affecting an estimated 5 percent of Americans under age eighteen. On the average every classroom in America has at least one student with ADD. An additional 6 million to 9 million American adults are thought to have ADD.

Many people with ADD or ADD **symptoms** have managed to live full and rewarding lives. Academy Award-winning actor Dustin Hoffman is among those who have been diagnosed with the disorder. A number of leaders from American history showed signs of ADD, from Benjamin Franklin, noted for his high-energy lifestyle, messiness, and countless projects and inventions, to Albert Einstein, a wild-haired genius who was expelled from school.

History of the Disorder

Attention deficit disorder has probably been around for centuries. There are plenty of tales of "bad" children who couldn't sit still, who were impulsive, and who always misbehaved. Dennis of the comic strip "Dennis the Menace" is just one example of a character who displays ADD traits.

Some cultures believed that the devil made children misbehave. Priests performed **exorcism** rites on them to try to free them from the devil's influence. Children whose bad behavior continued were often beaten and sometimes killed.

In more recent times, children with ADD have been expelled from school. They have been punished for their wild behavior, ridiculed, or called lazy.

Almost every classroom in America has a student with attention deficit disorder.

The picture hasn't been all bleak for people with ADD. Psychiatrist Edward Hallowell believes that many of the world's advances have been made by people with ADD. According to Hallowell, who himself has ADD, people with ADD tend to be impatient, impulsive, and drawn to risky behavior. But risk takers, he notes, are the very people who leave their homes to explore the world, who experiment, and who discover new ways of doing things.

George Frederic Still, a British doctor, first defined ADD behavior in children in 1902. He believed a brain injury or **defect** caused the behavior. Until then almost everyone thought children with ADD misbehaved on purpose. And most people blamed parents for not keeping their children under control.

The newly defined disorder was called **minimal brain dysfunction**. A brain dysfunction means that the brain doesn't work properly. By the 1930s a few doctors had begun giving **stimulants** to their patients with the disorder. A stimulant is a drug that arouses or speeds up the working of the brain. Surprisingly, this kind of drug helped children with the disorder to focus better. The disorder remained a mystery, however. No one could identify the brain injury or the defect that caused the symptoms. Many doctors continued to believe that poor parenting or a bad home life caused the uncontrollable behavior shown by certain children.

Hyperactivity and the Disorder

In 1960, scientific research added more evidence to show that this disorder was caused by a problem in the brain, though not necessarily by an injury. Because many of the children affected were much more active than others their age, researchers labeled them **hyperactive**. The disorder became known as the **hyperactive child syndrome**.

With further study, researchers in the 1960s and 1970s found that hyperactive children shared several traits:

1. They had trouble paying attention and finishing tasks. They often put off assignments until the last minute.
2. They were impulsive. They did or said things without thinking about the consequences. Many did not see how their actions affected other people or how others viewed them.
3. They overreacted. They had hot tempers or cried easily.

4. They wanted everything immediately. They didn't want to wait for rewards or results.

Because these children had such difficulty paying attention, the disorder was renamed attention deficit disorder in 1980.

Researchers used to believe that only children had ADD. They thought that the disorder disappeared as children grew older. In the 1980s and 1990s, however, studies revealed that adults, too, had many of the same ADD symptoms as children.

Researchers now believe that most children with ADD will continue to have symptoms when they become adults. Scientists estimate about 3 percent of the adult population has ADD. Many don't even know they have the disorder.

For many years only children who were hyperactive were thought to have ADD. For that reason the disorder was renamed **attention deficit hyperactivity disorder (ADHD)** in 1987. More recently, however, researchers have discovered that children who are not overly active may also have an attention deficit disorder. Like others with ADD, these children have a hard time paying attention. They are easily distracted by noises, conversations, and other activities. But instead of acting out, they daydream or "space out."

The term ADD now applies to both types of the disorder. ADHD is a form of ADD that also includes hyperactivity. Boys are more likely to be hyperactive, while girls tend to be the daydreamers. Both boys and girls, however, can have either form of attention deficit disorder.

Chapter 2

Symptoms

Babies who have attention deficit disorder may have trouble sleeping through the night. They are often restless and irritable. Rocking or moving in other ways may be the only way they can soothe themselves. And while all toddlers are active, those with ADD seem to have an inner motor that is always turned on. Like many children with ADD, Chris Prosser learned to walk early, when he was only eight months old. By the time he was two, he ran wherever he went and climbed on every available surface. His mother remembers that everything seemed to attract his attention.

People who have ADD get distracted easily. It is hard for them to pay attention. During class they may not be able to focus on what the teacher is saying. A bird flying outside the window may catch their attention. They may be distracted by another student who walks by the classroom door. A jagged fingernail or a crooked sock may draw their attention away from the lesson.

"If somebody I know has a conversation 20 yards down

the hallway, I'm going to listen in," says Chris. Diagnosed with ADHD when he was a sixth grader, Chris struggled for years to pay attention in class. But, with lots of work and help, he is overcoming his problems. Today, the six-foot, one-inch trombone player attends Berklee College of Music in Boston, Massachusetts.

It is hard for people with ADD to follow rules, to start projects and finish them, or to arrive on time. They often forget or disregard instructions. From the time Chris was a toddler, he paid no attention to orders or family rules. "No matter how many times you told him he couldn't do something," recalls Chris's mother, "he'd go ahead and do it."

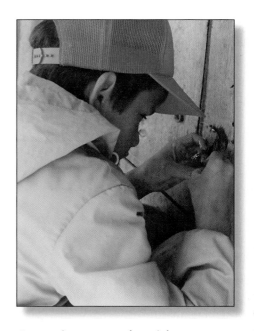

Sometimes people with attention deficit disorder become deeply engrossed in activities that interest them. Here, Chris puts a worm on a hook. He can fish for hours.

At times, however, people with ADD get so engrossed in a project that they tune out everything else. During these times they become super-focused. Chris remembers building a model sailboat for the Young America Cup competition for high-school students. He became so engrossed in the project that he lost all track of time. At midnight a school custodian found him working in the industrial arts room and told him to go home.

Chris waves from a rock above a swirling river. People with attention deficit disorder may engage in activities that are risky.

Risk Takers and Action Seekers

People with attention deficit disorder are impulsive. They often do things without thinking about the consequences. They are risk takers. Some participate in exciting activities, like skydiving or mountain climbing. Others take the lead in the school play and perform before an auditorium full of people. Sometimes their risk-taking behavior has negative effects: They might, for example, abuse alcohol or drugs or challenge the school bully. Instead of waiting their turn, children with ADD may push ahead in line or blurt out answers in class.

Like many people with ADD, Chris has injured himself several times because of his impulsive, risky behavior. A stick pierced Chris's leg after he jumped from a ledge into a sandpit. The injury required seventeen stitches and left a long scar on his leg. He also has dislocated his shoulder while skiing, smashed into a tree after driving his bicycle over a ramp, and burned his cheek with a flaming marshmallow. "At least," his mother says, "he's never injured anyone else."

Many people with ADD are hyperactive. A person who is hyperactive can't stay still. Such a person is always on the go, moving his or her fingers or feet, running instead of walking, chatting instead of listening. Sharon Prosser recalls one visit to the doctor's office when Chris was three or four. After Chris took off his shirt and pants, the doctor told him to lie on a table for an examination. The doctor turned to talk with Chris's mother. When they looked back at the table, it was empty. They found Chris in the waiting room, dressed in T-shirt and undershorts, excitedly stacking blocks.

Dreamers

Not all people with attention deficit disorder are hyperactive. Instead of fidgeting or misbehaving, they may stare off into space or daydream. Girls have this type of ADD more often than boys do.

Boys are two to three times more likely to be diagnosed as having ADD. This may be because boys with ADD are more likely than girls to be hyperactive. Everyone knows when they are not paying attention, because they usually disturb those who are. People may not notice when someone is quietly staring out the window.

"You're Not Trying Hard Enough"

Being impulsive, hyperactive, and easily distracted causes many problems for people with attention deficit disorder. In school, teachers often see them as troublemakers because they talk out of turn, can't sit still, and cause a commotion. Students with ADD may not be able to start or finish tests on time and often lose homework or forget to do it. Without help many students with ADD get behind in their studies. Teachers may think they're lazy or not trying hard enough. Parents say they're disappointed in them. Classmates and brothers and sisters often make fun of them.

A recent study found that teachers and parents were far more likely to criticize than praise a child with ADD. For every word of support a child with ADD received, he or she heard eight to nine negative remarks. With such criticism it's not surprising that many children with ADD soon begin to think of themselves as failures.

Chris remembers his teachers repeatedly telling him to try harder. "My teachers thought I was a slacker. They'd say, 'This is so easy; why can't you do it?' I didn't know."

Getting Along With Others

People with attention deficit disorder also may have trouble getting along with others. A boy or girl who often hits classmates or grabs balls away from other players does not win many friends. Sometimes people with ADD daydream while someone else is talking to them. This makes them seem uninterested in what the other person has to say. People with ADD may not notice that their behavior hurts others or makes them angry. Sharon Prosser says that Chris had no idea she would be frantic when he ran away to the beach. He just thought of it as an adventure.

On the other hand, a person with ADD can add spice to life. Chris may forget to meet his friends when he's supposed to, but once they get together, he keeps them laughing. "He's a lot of fun," says Sam Morrison, a childhood friend. "Everyone loves [Chris] Prosser. He always keeps us entertained."

Many children with ADD, however, have few friends and are lonely, frustrated, and angry. Some turn to drugs and alcohol for comfort or seek friends among other outcasts and get involved in crime. According to ADD expert Russell Barkley, as many as two-thirds of children with ADD become hostile and defiant by the time they are seven. An estimated 40 percent of hyperactive boys in one study had been arrested by the time they were eighteen. The juvenile justice system is clogged with children with ADD. Typical crimes include stealing and setting fires. Thomas Phelan, another ADD expert,

Chris Prosser, right, and his friend, Sam Morrison, enjoy toasted marshmallows in the summer of 1990.

estimates that 40 percent of those labeled as "problem children" have attention deficit disorder.

As adults, 25 to 30 percent of those diagnosed with ADD as children have problems with drugs and alcohol. Many experts believe that a large number of prison inmates have ADD that was never diagnosed when they were children.

Hard on Others, Hard on Themselves

Attention deficit disorder can be as hard on family, friends, and teachers as it is on the person with the disorder. Teachers may have to spend extra time and energy working with ADD students and keeping them from disrupting the rest of the class. Parents may have to be especially patient with children who have the disorder. They may have to watch over them much more closely than other children, making sure they do their homework and fulfill other duties.

Such constant attention can be exhausting. Brothers and sisters often resent a sibling who forgets to do his or her chores and who demands more of their parents' time. They also may be on the receiving end of angry outbursts, hitting, and other out-of-control behavior on the part of the sibling who has ADD.

Too often, children with ADD become scapegoats. They are blamed for everything that goes wrong in the family or in the classroom. If this goes on for long, children with ADD may soon believe that they are bad people.

The teen years can be especially difficult for children with ADD and their families. Lindy Holt, a chaplain who runs a support group for adults with ADD and has two sons with the disorder, says middle school can be particularly challenging. In elementary school, she notes, parents can work with one teacher to help the ADD student cope. Once a child enters middle school, however, parents have to deal with many teachers. Chances are likely that not all teachers will understand ADD or take the time to learn about the disorder. Teens want to make their own choices. They often object to having a parent make arrangements with teachers and school officials on their behalf.

"They don't want Mom around meddling," says Holt. She believes it is important to help teens with ADD accept responsibility for themselves.

During the teen years, students with ADD, like others their age, don't want to be different. Those who go to a special learning room or who need extra help often feel cut off from classmates who don't need such services. Sometimes other students make fun of them. Many teens with ADD have trouble making friends. "It's a tough age," Holt says.

Teens with ADD—frustrated with school and feeling left out—may express their anger by disrupting class, hitting others, or simply ignoring adults' instructions. Their rebellious behavior can escalate into violent or criminal acts that land them in jail.

C h a p t e r   3

Causes

Everything a person does, thinks, feels, believes, remembers, smells, sees, and hears begins in the brain. Every movement is controlled from the brain. The brain is the source of every emotion, thought, action, and reaction a person experiences. So just a small shift in the brain's workings can change the way a person behaves.

No one knows for sure exactly what causes attention deficit disorder. Many researchers believe ADD is caused by a biological problem in the brain. Most now agree that ADD is not the result of stubbornness, bad parenting, bad behavior, or stupidity. Except in rare cases of brain injury, people are born with attention deficit disorder.

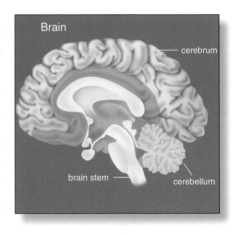

Many researchers believe attention deficit disorder is caused by a problem in the brain.

Some studies suggest that ADD is the result of a shortage of certain chemicals in the brain. For example, consider a boy shooting basketballs in physical education class. According to one scientific theory, a normally functioning brain releases a chemical called **dopamine** that controls impulses and signals the boy to wait his turn. But in someone with ADD, the theory suggests, not enough dopamine is released or absorbed by the brain. Without the message to be patient, this boy might grab the ball out of turn and get into trouble.

Children who have attention deficit disorder often have difficulty controlling their impulses. Because of this, others may not want to let them join in the fun.

From Parent to Child

Scientists doing research on the brain also have found clues that link attention deficit disorder to certain **genes**. Genes are tiny units in cells that determine each person's traits: hair color, height, even the ability to carry a tune. Many scientists believe that genes can also pass on traits which result in ADD. Each of us inherits our genes from our mother and father. More than one-third of parents with children diagnosed with ADD had the disorder themselves when they were children. The number may be even higher, since fewer people knew about ADD when today's parents were children. Researchers suggest that ADD is inherited in 90 to 95 percent of the cases.

Scientists have found that some people with ADD have a defect, or change, in a certain gene. In one study, 60 percent of people in the test group who had ADD had a defect in a gene tied to the chemical dopamine. Dopamine signals the brain to pay attention, among other things. Only 6 percent of those in the study who did not have ADD had a similar defect in that gene.

Too Many Messages

Other studies have shown that attention deficit disorder patients have less blood flowing to the front part of their brain than other people. That part of the brain screens the messages coming in, picks out the important ones, and determines which need a response. With less blood flowing to the frontal area, the brain slows down and can't sort through all the messages. That may explain why people with ADD have trouble focusing on one thing. It also may be why they often are drawn to risky behavior. Perhaps those messages that "make the most noise"—are the most intense—are the only ones that get noticed by the unfocused brain.

Physical differences also may be present in the brains of people with ADD. According to several research projects, a structure in the middle brain, called the **caudate nucleus**, is smaller than normal in some people with ADD. One role of this part of the brain is to start movement and control impulses. In other words, it lets a person know when to get started on a project and when to stop, when to say something and when to keep quiet.

Researchers are studying the brain to determine the causes of attention deficit disorder.

So far, none of these studies have led to one definite cause for ADD. It may be that several factors contribute to the disorder. One person may have ADD due to the lack of a certain chemical. A part of another person's brain may be smaller than normal. Still another person may have been born with a gene that causes ADD. Or a person may have all three factors.

Encephalitis, a flulike sickness that affects the brain, may, in rare cases, lead to ADD symptoms. Heavy use of alcohol by the mother during pregnancy, lead poisoning, and head injuries have also been linked to ADD. Despite some people's claims, there is no evidence that food allergies, food additives, sugar, or fluorescent lights cause attention deficit disorder.

Chapter 4

Diagnosis

Many people with attention deficit disorder do not learn they have the disorder until they are teenagers. Others may be adults before they are diagnosed. Some people never know they have ADD— just that they have a hard time focusing on projects or get into trouble often.

ADD can be hard to diagnose. People with ADD look the same as everyone else. There is no physical sign telling a doctor that a patient has ADD. Doctors can't determine if a person has ADD by testing the blood or by taking an X-ray of the brain.

A new test, however, may provide a safe way for doctors to diagnose ADD. Invented by Australian scientists, this test measures brain signals. In the test, children were asked to respond when they saw the letter X on a screen. The researchers looked at the children's brain waves while they were taking the test. In the children with ADD, the front part of the brain did not send out as many signals as it did in those of other children who took the test. More studies are needed, however, before doctors can routinely use the test on their patients.

Symptoms Tell the Story

Until the new test or others like it are available, the only way to learn if a person has attention deficit disorder is to look at the symptoms. Usually this requires a doctor or other expert who specializes in ADD. The first step, through the process of elimination, is to make sure the symptoms aren't caused by some other problem. A physical exam and blood tests check for illnesses and conditions that might produce the same symptoms as ADD. For example, a faulty **thyroid**, a gland that controls how active people are, can cause hyperactivity.

Sometimes, problems at home are to blame. A child who is abused may misbehave or be distracted. Someone who is depressed, on drugs, or anxious may not be able to focus on his or her schoolwork. Students whose parents have recently divorced or died may find their mind wandering in class.

Some children's symptoms are caused by a **learning disability**, not ADD. They may have trouble hearing or understanding what the teacher is saying. Others may have problems expressing themselves or simply may be confused by the lessons being taught. Some may have mental disorders that cause them to misbehave or tune out.

Once other problems have been ruled out, the expert will talk with the parents. Does the child have a hot temper? Is he or she overly active or always daydreaming? Does the child forget to do chores, have a messy room, and have

A tardy student hurries into school. A child's behavior at school can be a key in determining a diagnosis of attention deficit disorder.

trouble doing homework or lose it once it's done? How did the child behave as an infant and as a toddler? Is the child's behavior different from that of other children of the same age? Do the child's actions disturb other members of the family? Because ADD usually is inherited, the expert will ask if the mother, the father, or other relatives have the disorder.

Next is an interview with the child. Some children can talk quite clearly about their problems at school and at home. Others either don't want to discuss themselves or don't know what to say. Many show no signs of ADD in a doctor's office because it is new and interesting there. Often an expert will watch the child in school to see how he or she behaves.

Successes and Failures

One of the most valuable tools in diagnosing attention deficit disorder is a child's school record. The report cards of children with ADD are filled with remarks that give clues to the expert. Teachers may note that the child "talks too much in class"; "bothers classmates"; "needs to buckle down"; or "doesn't finish projects." Many children with ADD have an up-and-down school record. Often they excel in a subject, then fail the same subject the next term.

Chris's teachers "found him either very interesting or too much of a challenge," according to his mother. He shared wonderful ideas during class discussions, but he didn't complete his written work. Chris had trouble finishing his homework even when he understood the lessons. His friends took fifteen minutes to do the work, while he spent two hours and still didn't finish.

"I tried to get my homework done, but something else would pop into my head," Chris recalls. "All of a sudden it would be two hours later."

By the time Chris was in sixth grade, his mother decided to find out why he wasn't doing better in school. She asked the school to give Chris some tests.

Tests for Attention Deficit Disorder

Experts use questionnaires to help them decide if a person has attention deficit disorder. The **Conners Parents Questionnaire** has forty-eight questions on various behaviors. Parents mark which behaviors are a problem for their children. A similar form asks teachers to respond to twenty-eight questions about children's behavior at school. Russell Barkley also has written a questionnaire that explores behaviors at home and at school. Using the forms as a guide, the expert compares the child's behavior with that considered normal for children of the same age.

Tests are also given to the person who is thought to have ADD. The **Wechsler tests** measure people's intelligence in a number of ways. A tester asks a person to define words, to explain the relationship between words, and to solve math problems as quickly as possible.

In another part of the testing, people are asked to put blocks in the correct order to illustrate a story. These tests also measure people's short-term memory, their ability to concentrate, and how many numbers they can remember in sequence.

Like the rest of us, some people with ADD are very smart, others are average, and some have low intelligence. What sets them apart is that they often score much lower on written work than other people with the same abilities. Someone with Chris's intelligence normally would have scored higher on written tests he took to measure his math and other skills.

One third or more of children with ADD also have a learning disability. Learning disabilities make it harder for people to learn in a regular classroom. In addition to ADD, Chris has a problem with memory. Other learning disabilities may make reading difficult or math hard to understand. As part of the ADD screening, children often take tests to see whether they have a learning disability. Tests are not always accurate, however. That is because some children with ADD may get distracted while taking the test. Other students with ADD, however, may find the questions interesting and be able to focus on the answers.

Adults who think they have ADD go through a similar process. The expert doing the testing looks at school records, if they exist, and the person's work record. The expert also may talk with coworkers and family members. No special tests have been created for adults with ADD, but they can answer questions designed to detect the disorder.

As yet, there is no one test that proves someone has ADD. Because of this, some doctors think too many people are diagnosed with the disorder. They believe some children don't really have ADD at all but are just

Tests help determine if a person has attention deficit disorder.

very active or hard to control. Far fewer children are diagnosed with ADD in Europe than in the United States. Only one percent of children in England have been classed as hyperactive. ADD expert Edward Hallowell believes Americans are more likely to have ADD because they inherited the disorder from ancestors who were explorers and adventurers.

So, Who Has Attention Deficit Disorder?

Almost everyone has at least some ADD symptoms. In the United States, people live a fast-paced life every day. They flip from one television channel to another, rush to work,

People today live fast-paced lives, always rushing to meet the next appointment or flying to another city.

and get impatient if they have to wait in line. But not everyone has attention deficit disorder. Doctors believe only about 5 percent of Americans have the disorder. Those with ADD have symptoms that start in childhood and are often overpowering. The symptoms disrupt their lives and the lives of those around them. Without treatment these people might not be able to achieve all that they could otherwise.

Chapter 5

Treatments

Perhaps the worst side effect for those with attention deficit disorder is that too often children end up feeling bad about themselves. Without help they fall behind in school. They believe people who tell them that it is their fault they can't do the work. They think they are stupid or lazy or bad people. The truth is, of course, that attention deficit disorder prevents them from being able to focus on their lessons.

One-third to one-half of children with ADD must repeat one or more grades in school. A third don't graduate from school. Many have trouble making friends, become involved in fights, and have to endure scoldings and punishments. Some abuse drugs and spend time in jail.

There is no cure for ADD. Some people with the disorder become less active and are able to focus better on a job they like as they grow older. For most, however, ADD symptoms will remain with them for life. Adults with ADD may find jobs where their disorder is not a problem.

Some learn to live with ADD. Many people find that treatment helps them live happier, more productive lives.

Education

The first step in any treatment plan is education. Learning about ADD can make it much easier for those who have the disorder. They can use aids to help them stay focused and avoid situations that will distract them.

Chris Prosser found it was easier for him to learn his lessons by viewing videos and flash cards than by listening to a lecture. Other people with attention deficit disorder use calculators and computers to help them learn and finish tasks on time.

Once teachers and parents learn about ADD, they, too, can take steps to help children with the disorder. A teacher showed Chris how to take notes and study better. Some students with ADD may need extra time to finish tests. Special education classes can help those with learning disabilities, as well as students whose ADD interferes with their learning.

As a middle-school student, Chris entered the special education program at his school. That meant he had classes with a small group of other students who had problems with learning. "I didn't want to be there," Chris says. "I missed my friends and was afraid they would make fun of me."

Chris soon discovered he liked the small classes. "It really helped," he says. Chris learned much more when a teacher was on hand to answer his questions and get him back on track when his attention wandered. He also found that his friends were interested in ADD and asked him questions about the disorder. "Everybody can relate to ADD," Chris says, "because everybody has a little bit of the symptoms." Experts say it's important to let classmates know about ADD so they don't think a student is getting special favors.

Learning about ADD also can help those with the disorder begin to like themselves better. After many years of blaming themselves, they learn that much of their "bad" behavior in the past resulted from ADD. At first, Chris didn't tell anybody about his ADD diagnosis. "I was afraid people might think I was using it as an excuse," he says. After talking with an ADD expert, though, Chris realized that many of his problems in school could be explained by ADD. "I was kind of relieved to learn that I was trying, just like everyone else."

Computers can help students with attention deficit disorder finish their work on time.

Counseling

Despite lectures from teachers and parents, Chris never lost his joy of living. His sense of humor and his enthusiasm won him many friends. He served as class treasurer, placed among the best in the state in golf, and excelled in floor hockey and skiing. His high-school team placed second in the state in the Young America Cup model boat-building competition. Chris's work with other students on the boat project taught him how to get along better with people.

"I learned how to work on a team," Chris says. "Before this, I had always wanted to be in charge."

Most of all, Chris's music lifted his spirits. "When he played his trombone," his mother says, "Chris could shine."

Chris Prosser receiving an award for his work on the Young America Cup boat-building competition.

Even with his upbeat attitude, Chris found it helpful to talk with a counselor. At the sessions, Chris talked about how ADD affected his life. The counselor helped Chris set up a homework schedule that allowed time to relax. Some people with ADD think so badly of themselves that they need help from a counselor to raise their self-esteem. Others seek help in dealing with their anger and hostile feelings. A counselor can teach them how to get along better with other people. Sometimes the entire family may need help in dealing with attention deficit disorder. People with ADD often benefit from support groups, where they can share their problems and feelings with others who also have the disorder.

Behavior Training

Behavior training can also help people with attention deficit disorder. Under this system, children learn new ways to do things and receive rewards for good behavior. A boring task becomes much more interesting when it is tied to a special treat. Chris's parents posted a plan on the refrigerator that outlined the behavior they wanted Chris to follow. Each time Chris followed the plan, his parents awarded him points he could cash in to buy a special treat. Chris eventually earned enough points to buy a remote control car.

A similar plan is often used at school. Children in lower grades may receive a star for following their behavior plan. At the end of the day or the week, children who have earned a certain number of stars receive a special treat, such as selecting a gift from a prize box. Parents may reward good behavior by buying children an ice cream cone or allowing them to have a friend come to visit. Older children, like Chris, may be rewarded with money or special privileges, such as driving the family car.

Structure and Memory Aids

Structure is especially important for people with attention deficit disorder. They need to set up a routine for everyday activities. That helps them remember to do things on time and cuts down on distractions. The plan for a typical day may list times for getting up, eating breakfast, catching the bus, doing homework, playing with friends, and going to bed. People with ADD also may set aside a certain place to study. For some that means working in silence. Others do better if music or television plays in the background.

To help remember things, people with ADD often need to mark the calendar, keep a logbook, and write lists and notes to jog their memories. One young woman had notes posted throughout the house. It may have looked strange to a visitor, but it helped her remember the tasks she had to do. Chris kept track of his high-school schedule by listing each chore in a planning book every day.

Medication

By the time he reached high school, Chris did better with his lessons, but he still had trouble getting his work done on time. A doctor suggested he try **Ritalin**, the drug taken most often by people with attention deficit disorder.

Medication helps three-quarters of those with the disorder, making a big difference in their lives. It calms them down and makes them far less impulsive. They can pay attention in class and at work. They begin to relate to other people better.

Dr. Hallowell says medication helps an ADD patient in the same way that glasses help a person who is nearsighted. Both help the person focus better.

Ritalin (**methylphenidate**) and **Dexedrine** (**dextro-amphetamine**) are the most common drugs prescribed for

ADD. **Cylert (magnesium pemoline)** is another drug used for ADD. All three are stimulants, drugs that make the brain more active. Scientists are not sure how the drugs work, but they seem to increase the amounts of certain chemicals in the brain.

Chris found that Ritalin helped him tune out many of the things that had distracted him. "I can finally hear the teacher instead of the fan in the back of the room," he told his mother after he took the drug for the first time. At the end of his freshman year of high school, Chris's grades had improved so much that he moved into a high-level science class and a regular English class. He still struggled with math, though, and returned to the resource room for study hall.

When he takes Ritalin, Chris says, "I want to get this energy out of my brain and get it down on paper." The medication helps him focus on one task. "I can get it done and move onto the next task rather than try to deal with everything at once," he says. Chris continues to take Ritalin while attending Berklee College of Music in Boston.

Chris has had few problems with Ritalin. Some people, however, have trouble sleeping, lose their appetite, or feel drugged when they take the medicine. Others have stomachaches or feel nervous. Usually these side effects stop after a few days or when the dose is lowered. Children may stop growing while taking Ritalin, but they start growing again during short breaks from the medicine.

A dose of the drug lasts about four hours. Most children take a pill at breakfast and again during lunch. This can be a problem for those who forget to take the second dose. The school nurse usually distributes medication to

Checking in periodically with a coach—a teacher, parent, or adult friend—can help keep a student with attention deficit disorder on track.

students during the school year. For those not in school and who forget to take a lunchtime dose, a longer-acting pill taken once a day can be used. But it may not work as well for some people.

When stimulants don't help, people with ADD may try other types of medication. An **antidepressant** can help some people with ADD become calmer and less angry. The medication, used in higher doses for depression, lasts longer than stimulants. Usually people take a pill once a day or in the morning and at bedtime. Like stimulants these drugs increase the levels of certain chemicals in the brain. They don't work as well as stimulants in helping people focus.

Other drugs also may be used to treat ADD. In general,

they calm people and help them cope better. Some people may require more than one drug to treat the disorder.

About one-quarter of people with ADD are not helped by medication or can't take it because of side effects. They must use methods such as behavior training, structure, lists, and other aids to deal with ADD.

Coaching

Just as players on a team benefit from advice from their coach, a coach also can help people with attention deficit disorder stay on track. People with ADD can arrange for a counselor, a teacher, or a friend to serve as a coach. Once both sides have agreed to the arrangement, the coach and the person with ADD set up goals and tasks that have to be completed. Then the coach checks in with the person every week or so to make sure the goals are being met. The coach also can serve as a cheerleader, praising the person for successes and urging him or her to keep trying.

When he was in high school, Chris Prosser reported to a teacher every day on the homework he had to do. The teacher checked his progress and made sure he was studying. With a push from the teacher, Chris managed to finish most of his homework on time.

Chapter 6

Living With
Attention Deficit
Disorder

A ttention deficit disorder can bring both tears and joy to those who have the disorder. In many cases the same traits that cause problems for people with ADD can bring them rewards. Risky behavior common among those with ADD can cause injuries and sometimes even death. But people willing to try new things also can invent useful devices, solve problems, and create beautiful artwork. Risk takers are often the ones to start successful businesses.

Thinking about several things at once can make it hard to focus. But it can also help a person to be creative. "I always have three or four thoughts running through my mind at once," Chris says.

By drawing on all those ideas floating through his brain, Chris notes that he often writes a song a week "when I can get myself to sit down for ten minutes." The high energy that got him into trouble in elementary school now helps him.

There are still struggles for Chris, as there are for most people with ADD. Teens with ADD, like other people their age, want to be independent. But that becomes difficult when schools do not allow students to take the ADD medication on their own. A school nurse or other official must dole out the pills.

Chris Prosser loves playing his trombone. He says attention deficit disorder helps him be more creative.

On the other hand, teens who want to use drugs to get high may ask students with ADD to share their medication. One girl gave her ADD pills to other students in an effort to make friends. Lindy Holt notes that her son once handed out pills to some older ninth-grade friends.

Even after being diagnosed with ADD, people often find that others don't believe they have a disorder. "If you're not physically handicapped, with a cane or a wheelchair, people don't understand," says Mrs. Prosser.

Some teachers at Chris's high school refused to let him use a calculator or other aids in class. "They thought he would do fine if he just studied harder and applied himself," says his mother.

Chris hasn't told all his college professors he has ADD. His trombone teacher, however, can tell from his behavior when he hasn't taken his Ritalin. Chris says the hardest thing about having ADD "is to remember to take my pill." He takes Ritalin with his meals—as long as he eats on schedule. Chris doesn't like to think of himself as "someone who needs help." But he admits that the structure and the medication have helped "a tremendous amount."

"It's not such a bad thing," he says of ADD. "I can see things differently from other people. I'm a lot less restricted in my creativity, and it comes out in my horn."

Further Reading

Barkley, Russell. *Attention Deficit Hyperactivity Disorder: A Handbook for Diagnosis and Treatment.* New York: Guilford Publications, Inc., 1998.

Dwyer, Kathleen M. *What Do You Mean I Have ADD?* New York: Walker & Co., 1996.

Gordon, Michael. *I Would If I Could: A Teenager's Guide to ADHD–Hyperactivity.* DeWitt, N.Y.: GSI Publications, 1993.

———. *Jumpin' Johnny: Get Back to Work! A Child's Guide to ADHD-Hyperactivity.* DeWitt, N.Y.: GSI Publications, 1991.

———. *My Brother's a World-Class Pain: A Sibling's Guide to ADHD–Hyperactivity.* DeWitt, N.Y.: GSI Publications, 1992.

Hallowell, Edward M., M.D., and John J. Ratey, M.D. *Driven to Distraction: Recognizing and Coping with Attention Deficit Disorder from Childhood Through Adulthood.* New York: Simon & Schuster Trade, 1995.

Harris, Jacqueline. *Learning Disorders.* New York: Twenty-First Century Books, 1995.

Levine, Mel, M.D. *Keeping a Head in School.* Cambridge, Mass.: Educators Publishing Service, 1996.

Moragne, Wendy. *Attention Deficit Disorder.* Brookfield, Conn.: Millbrook Press, 1996.

Morrison, Jaydene. *Coping with ADD–ADHD.* New York: Rosen Publishing Group, 1995.

Nadeau, Kathleen G., and Ellen B. Dixon. *Learning to Slow Down and Pay Attention: A Book for Kids About ADD.* Washington, D.C.: American Psychological Association, 1998.

Quinn, Patricia O., M.D. *Adolescents and Attention Deficit Disorder: Gaining the Advantage.* Washington, D.C.: American Psychological Association, 1995.

Quinn, Patricia O., M.D., and Judith Stern. *Putting on the Brakes.* Skokie, Ill.: Educational Publishing Foundation Book, 1991.

Vail, Priscilla. *Smart Kids With School Problems: Things to Know and Ways to Help.* New York: Penguin, 1988.

———. *Learning Styles: Food for Thought and 130 Practical Tips.* Rosemont, N.J.: Modern Learning Press, 1992.

———. *Emotion: The On/Off Switch for Learning.* Rosemont, N.J.: Modern Learning Press, 1994.

For More Information

The following is a list of organizations, newsletters, tapes, and Web sites that deal with attention deficit disorder.

Organizations

Attention Deficit Information Network
475 Hillside Ave., Needham, MA 02194;
(781) 455-9895; <http://www.addinfonetwork.com>

Children and Adults with Attention Deficit Disorders
8181 Professional Place, Suite 201, Landover, MD 20785; (800) 233-4050

Equal Employment Opportunity Commission
1401 L St., N.W., Washington, D.C. 20507;
(202) 663-4900; <http://www.eeoc.gov>

Learning Disabilities Association of America
4156 Library Rd., Pittsburgh, PA 15234;
(412) 341-1515; <http://www.ncld.org>

National Attention Deficit Disorder Association
1788 Second St., Suite 200, Highland Park, IL 60035;
(847) 432-ADDA

National Center for Learning Disabilities
381 Park Ave. S., Suite 1401, New York, NY 10016;
(212) 545-7510

Self-Help Clearing House
St. Claire's Riverside Medical Center, Pocono Road, Denville, NJ 07834; (201) 625-9565

Newsletters

CH.A.D.D.ER. A semiannual publication of Children and Adults with Attention Deficit Disorders (CH.A.D.D.), see address and phone, p. 43

Focus. Quarterly newsletter of the National Attention Deficit Disorder Association, see address and phone, p. 43

Audiotapes and Videotapes

A.D.D. WareHouse. Audiotapes and videotapes on ADD; (800) 233-9273/(954) 792-8944; <http://www.addwarehouse.com/indexc.htm>

Barkley, Russell, Ph.D. *ADHD: What Do We Know?* and *ADHD: What Can We Do?* Guilford Press Videos, Guilford Publications Inc., 72 Spring St., New York, NY 10012; (800) 365-7006; <http://www. guilford.com>

Phelan, Thomas W. *All About Attention Deficit Disorder.* Child Management Inc., 1990; (800) 442-4453; Child Abuse Hot Line, press option #1

Internet Resources

<http://www.ADD.IDsite.com>
Lists lots of links to other sites and includes tips to build self-esteem.

<http://www.add.org>
Operated by National Attention Deficit Disorder Association (ADDA). Information on ADD, list of assessment services, monthly newsletter.

<http://www.cadvision.com/pchoate/links.htm>
Links to many other sites dealing with ADD.

<http://www.chadd.org>
Operated by Children and Adults with Attention
Deficit Disorders (C.H.A.D.D.). Much information
on ADD, plus a list of support groups nationwide.

<http://www.psych.org/public_info/read_kidsadd.html>
List of books on ADD prepared by the American
Psychiatric Association.

<http://wellweb.com/INDEX/QADD.HTM>
Lots of information on ADD, medications, research,
and other resources from the Wellness Web.

<http://www.kidshealth.org/kid/feeling/adhdkid.html>
Information about ADD oriented to kids. Created by
The Alfred I. duPont Hospital for Children, The
Nemours Children's Clinics, and other children's
health facilities nationwide.

<http://www.educ.indiana.edu/cas/adol/mental.html>
Adolescence Directory On-Line (ADOL) provides
links to information on adolescent issues; a service of
the Center for Adolescent Studies at Indiana
University.

Glossary

antidepressant—A medication used to treat ADD; in higher doses, it is used to treat depression.

attention deficit disorder (ADD)—A condition in which the brain doesn't focus as it should, making it hard for people with the disorder to pay attention.

attention deficit hyperactivity disorder (ADHD)—A type of ADD in which the patient also is hyperactive (*see below*).

behavior training—A method of teaching people to behave in new ways by offering rewards for good behavior.

caudate nucleus—A structure in the middle brain that signals the body to begin moving or to control impulses; it is smaller than normal in some people with ADD.

Conners Parents Questionnaire—A series of questions asked of parents to determine if their child has ADD.

Cylert—The brand name of magnesium pemoline, a stimulant used to treat ADD.

defect—The lack of a necessary part or a malfunctioning part that causes a system to work incorrectly.

Dexedrine—The brand name of dextroamphetamine, one of the most common stimulants used to treat ADD.

dextroamphetamine—*See* Dexedrine.

dopamine—A chemical in the brain that helps a person focus or pay attention.

encephalitis—A disease affecting the brain that can lead to ADD symptoms.

exorcism—A ceremony performed to drive away the devil or other evil spirits.

genes—Tiny units within each cell that determine a person's traits.

hyperactive—Overactive, unable to stay still.

hyperactive child syndrome—A term used for ADD beginning in 1960, referring to children who were overactive.

learning disability—A problem with hearing, vision, or other function that makes it hard for a person to learn in a regular classroom.

magnesium pemoline—*See* Cylert.

methylphenidate—*See* Ritalin.

minimal brain dysfunction—A term first used for ADD, referring to a brain defect or minor problem with the brain.

Ritalin—The brand name of methylphenidate, the most common medication used to treat ADD; a stimulant.

stimulants—Drugs that make the brain more active; often used to treat ADD.

symptom—A sign of disease or a behavior caused by a disease or disorder; for example, a sneeze may be a symptom of a cold or allergy.

thyroid—A gland located in the neck that regulates a person's activity level.

Wechsler tests—A series of tests used to measure intelligence; often given with other tests to help determine whether a child has ADD.

Index